Motor Touring in Old California

Motor Touring in Old California

Picturesque Ramblings with Auto Enthusiasts

Don DeNevi
and
Thomas Moulin

with photographs from the
Moulin Studios
in San Francisco and
the Railway Negative Exchange

279527

CELESTIAL ARTS
Millbrae, CA

Copyright © 1979 by Don DeNevi and Thomas Moulin

Celestial Arts
231 Adrian Road
Millbrae, California 94030

First printing, March 1979

Manufactured in the United States of America

Cover design by Robert Hu
Interior design by Abigail Johnston

Library of Congress Cataloging in Publication Data

DeNevi, Donald P.
　　Motor touring in old California.

　　1.　California—Description and travel—1951—
Guide-books.　　2.　automobiles—Road guides—
California.　　I.　Moulin, Tom, 1929-　　joint author.
II. Title.
F859.3D46 1979　　917.94'04'05　　78-67851
ISBN 0-89087-234-1

1 2 3 4 5 6 7　—　85 84 83 82 81 80 79

Contrary to all Norman's high hopes and exaggerated expectations, this book is NOT dedicated to his new Morgan, that little propane-propelled runabout. Instead, Motor Touring is dedicated with warmth and affection to the old man's son and daughter, Kenneth Norman and Sara Jane, two Alfa Romeo enthusiasts, if there ever were any. . .

Don DeNevi

Contents

Seeing California With a Babymobile

by Gus Anthony

Motoring in California, land of dreaming,
  Where the moonlight filters sweetly
  Through the oak trees in the canyons,
    is a pleasure beyond words.
Pendant from the silver heaven
Stars as jewels gleam and glistens;
Drowsily the forest creatures
  Upon hearing my motor's rumble
softly patter through the grasses,
Where the lulling insect-humming
Mutes its harshness as well as the brook's
  melodious singing.
Sliding o'er the blue-gray granite
Freshening waters seek the valleys;
There the towering eucalyptus
Guards the groves of fragrant orange,
And the weary cities slumber
by the ocean called Pacific.

Motoring in California, land of sun and shade,
  Where the humble people work and play
  Through their cities and valleys,
    is a pleasure just before heaven.

"Babymobile, let's go!"

STALKING his prey with the stealth of a hunter, he aimed not a weapon, but his fragile automobile. With considerable enthusiasm, he pointed it quickly and precisely down dirt or paved roads, most less than ideally suited for four wheel use. Fearless adventurers such as this fellow wanted to experience the fullness of California scenery, unspoiled and uncrowded, scenic and vast, where it was still possible to see the forests for the trees.

Before 1907, the automobile was considered the supreme luxury and every owner a Croesus. Prices were certainly on a grand scale, with, for example, a small acetylene headlight costing over $50. No matter that nine out of ten times it exploded like a cannon whenever one put a match to it. But in those days the horseless carriage was a wonderful and dazzling object greatly admired. By 1911, that same acetylene headlight cost less than $3.00. In fact, cars were not only cheaper, but gave less trouble and offered more genuine, care-free satisfaction than the $12,000 imported Eastern beauties.

Not only were the automobiles improving every year, but so were the archenemies of every motorist in the state: the roads. By 1912, road conditions all over California had improved to an extraordinary degree. A year before, the citizens of the state voted $18,000,000 for new and improved roads. Every town was to be the focus of the "good roads

Introduction

movement." Chambers of Commerce could boast to their Eastern brothers and sisters, "Look at our roads!", instead of asking them to admire their giant prunes or Brobdingnagian potatoes.

California, the ideal touring ground for America, as well as the rest of the world, was at last being fully opened. No state in the union offered greater variety of scenery for the tourist than the Golden State. In the interior valleys, he could find long stretches of level road where he could "let her out" for an exhilarating spin. The key lure, other than the scenery, however, was California's weather. In Europe, or on America's Eastern Coast, summers were either hot, humid, or cold. Europe, moreover, had its vexing custom houses, its pettyfogging restrictions and regulations, its graft, impositions, bothersome foreign languages, *and* rain. Eastern America, though often picturesque and historical, was not only intensely hot, but unleashed billions of mosquitoes that made changing a tire impossible. Green-headed horseflies, as well as innumerable other insects, added to the misery, buzzing and biting with maddening ferocity.

In California, however, one could travel during the Spring and Summer months along roads bordering orchards in full bloom or along vast, open grain fields growing in deep yellows. During the Autumn, the motorist could observe almost every vegetable product as they matured in their well- cared for rows. If he was a lover of the mountains, he could find the Coast Range or the Sierras in almost every county. Or, if he were a true enthusiast in search of grades which would test the hill climbing powers of his little machine, or deep sand that would test his temper and patience, he was within hours of these as well. To those who arrived first, there was little question of the endless miracle of California.

Lloyd Osbourne, author of such titles as *The Motor-Maniacs* and *Motor Adventuring,* said,

> Any stranger bringing his car to California should take his chauffeur aside, and speak to him something like this: "William, I am afraid you are not going to get much pleasure out of this trip, and I wish to prepare you for some things that will displease and shock you. We intend, for instance, to start every morning *as late as we like;* we shall not have the slightest concern as to how few miles we make a day; we are capable of stopping the car for a whole half hour at a time *just to admire the scenery;* we may even get out our rods and go fishing up some mountain brook quite regardless of your speedometer, or your natural impatience; we mean to dawdle through California, soaking in all the charm and beauty of it; if night should overtake us unawares we shall spread our blankets under a tree and sleep like hobos."

William, of course, will be very much upset. To stop his car for anything short of a puncture or a blow-out is an outrage to a chauffeur's feelings. His dream of perfect bliss is a mathematically-straight French road and forty miles an hour—with you holding your hair on while the landscape cinematographs by in a pale-green blur. This is William's idea of touring, and the sooner he is broken of it in California the better. You will sink in his esteem, but you must brace up to that and try to meet it like a man. Always remember that after all it is *you* who are paying William, and that—when it comes down to the eternal verities—it is *your* car.

Thus did Easterners see the scenic potentialities of motoring in the West. With new fast-flying machines usurping the place of the bronco, stage coach, and prairie schooner, California, the land of gold and sunshine, became the new mecca for every tourist who knew how to drive.

In 1907, there were less than 300 registered automobiles in the entire state. In that pioneering year when the car was still young, the "horseless carriage" was permitted to use only certain roads and streets and allowed to travel only eight or ten miles an hour (if it could indeed go that fast).

By 1910, there were more than 1,000 autos registered in California. Ten years later, the number jumped to almost 14,000. However, the arrival of touring cars from out of the state was at least four times this number. Because of the increase in the use of automobiles throughout America and the extension of highway systems leading to the Golden State, coupled with the ever-spreading fame of the Pacific Coast region, motor tourists were entering the 19 major gates into California at the rate of 54,000 a year by 1920.

The philosophy of virtually every one of these early motorists was that his touring automobile was a "little yacht on wheels." Armed with his provisions and equipment, maps and compass, and eager consultations with fellow mariners, he would embark along the state's highways and byways. The motorist felt he could "sail up to a hotel and if he did not like its looks sail away again, with no more concern as to where he would finally lay his head than a tramp."

But like the sailor, the hardy and adventurous motorist was totally dependent on good weather. For this reason, California stood out as the happiest of the happy hunting grounds. As one Chamber of Commerce put it, "The state has a diversity of natural beauty that cannot be excelled—a sparkling freshness, picturesqueness and individuality that win the stranger's heart and make the native born Californian talk in superlatives. It is really only the meadowlark who can adequately convey the spirit of this exquisite land. Do come and visit us. We are waiting for you."

During the first two decades of this century, the auto enthusiast's royal road in California was El Camino Real. The foot-path of the early padres had been transformed into a luxurious boulevard by the taxes of the multitude for whom their adventurous zeal blazed away. By 1914, this Highway of the King upon which some $18,000,000 had been lavished ran north and south, from Mexico to Oregon, forming a main and permanent artery of nearly 1,000 miles in length. More than this, it was part of a rapidly shaping dream that would make the highway continuous through Oregon and Washington an international avenue along the coast of the Pacific, from Mexico to Canada. El Camino Real was to be all its name implied: a royal road. In fact, Governor Gillett said in his second biennial message to the legislature, "The work of building this state highway shall be most carefully planned and considered so that when completed it will compare favorably with the best roads of Europe and of this country." This ensured to the motor tourist not only absolute safety, long stretches of hard levels, and gentle gradients even over the ruggedest mountains, but a road that would be open the whole year round, and as good for touring in December as in June.

For example, one departing from San Diego along El Camino Real would look toward the Cuyamaca mountains and northward to the San Bernardino mountains with their snowy peaks overlooking the sea and the vast sunny panorama of the orange country. If one left the royal road and headed toward the dazzling summits of those ranges, he would pass through more than a dozen climates. From the orange country the road led north along the level heart of the long state, following in the footsteps of the padres. He would pass one quaint old mission after another, peacefully slumbering in their scents of rose blossoms. Then, the traveler would pass through Los Angeles, city of homes, with her charming companies of bungalows spreading from mountains to beaches; Santa Barbara, the ancient capital, with its country clubs, golf links, ever-blooming gardens and animated fashionable life; Paso Robles, the land of spreading oaks and curative waters and on to Monterey and the loveliest coast scenery of the world. Here, he would find the incredible Seventeen Mile Drive, the old Carmel Mission, where once a year a service was still held within its crumbling walls. In nearby Monterey, the tourist could walk through the venerable adobe house where the Stars and Stripes were first hoisted over California and pause to smell the scents from General Sherman's still-surviving rose-bush. If he were so inclined, the auto enthusiast could indulge in some of the best and most varied sea-fishing to be found on the Pacific.

Turnbull Canyon Road,
San Gabriel Valley

Continuing north to San Francisco, the traveller would drive along level roads stretching past San Juan and its immense nurseries of sweet peas "filling the air with the most exquisite fragrance under heaven." Through the Santa Clara valley, his little auto would fly. To the right and left would be found tempting orchards of prunes, peaches, and apricots, a wilderness of blossoms in the early spring. Perhaps, this adventurous tourist would decide to take a byway to Santa Cruz in order to visit its immense pleasure palace and bathing beach. From there, he could head for San Francisco through the mountain grades of Soquel and the Big Trees of the Santa Cruz Mountains. At San Jose, the tourist might pause to inspect the greatest of all telescopes in the observatory on the summit of Mount Hamilton. Under it rested the body of James Lick, the millionaire who built and endowed it. From San Jose, it was a short jaunt to Stanford University, one of the world's great learning centers. There he could pause in this inspiring citadel in order to inspect the interesting old Spanish style of architecture. Or, if he were so inclined, he could swing around the eastern side of the great bay of San Francisco, through small villages bordering

An early visitor to the top of
Mt. Roubidoux in Riverside

the long stretch of road. Upon arriving in Oakland, the motorist could either visit the University of California in nearby Berkeley or take the ferry across the bay waters to the San Francisco metropolis. San Francisco was indeed a sight for the enthusiastic motor tourist. Known as the Exposition City because she was the world's host in 1915, San Francisco was a city of precipitous streets, glorious parks, famed Presidio, and a vantage point for inspiring views of the Golden Gate, Mount Diablo, that grim mountain of once a thousand boiling springs and sulphurous exhalations, and Mount Tamalpais, across the Bay in Marin County, which could be circled by motor in one delightful ten-hour period.

From the Bay Area to the San Joaquin Valley and Sacramento, the highway carried one through interminable marshes, most of which were teeming with wild duck. The area just east of Mount Diablo was a region of picturesque desolation, spacious, vast, and silent, with an occasional shooting-box set in the ooze and tule. Once in Sacramento, the Golden State's capital, the tourist could visit the spot where gold was discovered. From there, the eager motorist had a choice of three possible scenic trips: north into Shasta County and into Oregon; south and east to San Andreas County; and northeast to Lake Tahoe. During any time of the year, the three routes provided the motorist with scenery so spectacular that it was unmatched anywhere in the world.

For example, if he decided to head for southern Oregon, the sojourner would wind his little automobile through mountains and forest of almost primeval grandeur abounding in every variety of game. Yet, along the way, he would find great hotels and restaurants which provided all the quiet leisure and good eating any metropolis could offer. If he headed for the Bret Harte country, he would ride through Jackson, San Andreas, Sonora, Columbia, Bridgeport to the veritable Alps of California, the great Yosemite. If he chose to ride to Lake Tahoe, he would travel the stage-road once used by the Pony Express. Placerville and its historic relics were a must for the auto enthusiast. No matter which way he drove, a more exhilarating country could not be found. With "air like champagne, park-like forests carpeted with pine-needles, and innumerable streams and lakes full of darting trout," California was indeed worthy of her reputation. What entranced the autoist the most was the fact that often it would be 80° in the shade and he could still see the patches of snow glistening in the clefts of the Sierra rocks.

Delightful side trips north of San Francisco could readily be had. For instance, one could drive through the transplanted Italy of the Napa vineyards and into the mountain vastness of Lake County dotted with her healing mineral springs. Clear Lake was especially lovely with citrus fruits blossoming all around her edges.

From San Francisco north to Eureka, the journey was one through 200 miles of virgin redwoods, almost all of the only forest of its kind in the entire world.

As Lloyd Osbourne remarked,

> For the timid or ultra-conservative, El Camino Real offers one of the great opportunities of the world—level going for hundreds of miles through scenes of changing beauty and in equable weather. For the motorist who cares to take the chances that lie off level roads, there is equal opportunity in this land of natural wonders. He should be warned that the grades are often severe, the roads narrow and winding, and that a cool head and powerful brakes are much to be recommended.
>
> Speaking of brakes, it is a pity the ordinary driver does not use his gears more in making very steep descents. A car that is put into the "low," with the power turned off, can descend almost anything in absolute safety. Apart from sometimes saving people's lives, this also saves brake-linings, and obviates the frequent necessity in a mountain country of "taking up" your brakes. The passengers, too, instead of holding their breath and speculating on the imminence of eternity can thus gain some enjoyment from the scenes they are passing through. It is also well in California to equip yourself with a pair of big wooden blocks, and keep them handy on the floor of the dash. If you should be stopped on some wild grade let someone jump off and quickly block the rear wheels. In a pinch it is not always easy to find stones

for this purpose. A two-ton car is a pesky animal to stop when once it begins to roll the wrong way.

Returning to San Francisco, the automobile tourist would find many available roads open for motoring. However, in only one direction (to the south) could the automobilist make an extended run. If he chose to drive in any other direction, he had to transport his machine by ferry to either Oakland, Tiburon, or Sausalito. However, if the motorist remained in the city, and if he were the happy possessor of a license issued after the exam into his fitness to control his mechanically propelled carriage, there were endless nooks and crannies to explore. The Presidio reservation, for example, offered several excellent roads with views. He could then head south on 19th Avenue to Ingleside. By 1907, the roads in San Mateo, Burlingame, Mayfield, and Menlo Park were as good as any to be found in the United States. Henry Chisholm who travelled throughout California in his Packard Touring Car commented, "I must say the roads are much better than my best expectations. The condition of the roads in general is very much better than that of the roads in New England. And, the village councils have not gotten the foolish idea that automobiles have no right to travel in their villages. All the inhabitants along the country roads will do anything to assist one."

The first automobile in San Francisco was owned by Charles Fair, who had a strongly-developed mania for fast traveling. Tragically, this mania cost him and his wife their lives. Like his powerful launch "Lucero," Fair's motor car was of the gasoline type. Then, he bought an electric automobile. A few months before his death in Paris, Fair brought to San Francisco a fine racing machine, the product of the famous Panhard-Levassor factory, as well as a Parisian chauffeur to operate it. With the exception of Fair's two motorcars, almost all the cars owned in California were steam carriages manufactured by the Locomobile, Mobile, or White companies. A gasoline touring car was almost unknown and nearly all the vehicles were "light run-abouts."

Charles Baldwin owned a Panhard-Levassor automobile with four cylinders, which from its color, if not from its disposition and performances, was known as "Yellow Devil." Upon its arrival in San Francisco, it had hot tube ignition. A while later, it was fitted with an electric spark apparatus, thus making it capable of a higher rate of speed than any other motor-car in California.

By 1908, the steam carriages (except for heavy passenger service and livery work for which they were especially well adapted) were dropping out of favor. They were being supplanted by gasoline cars, most of the well-known manufacturers having dealers in San Francisco. Of these, the best known were the Winton Touring Car, the Packard, the Oldsmobile, the Cadillac, the St. Louis, the Haynes-Apperson, the Auto-Car, the Peerless, and the Toledo. The first owner of a Winton Touring Car in California was W.H. Talbot, who was a noticeable figure at the runs of the San Francisco Automobile Club in 1907. Among the wealthy owners of the famous 1903 Winton Touring Car were F.A. Hyde, the President of the Automobile Club of California, Mrs. Phoebe A. Hearst, R.P. Schwerin, M.H. De Young, Charles C. Moore, G.P. Fuller, Sydney Starr, Templeton Crocker, J. Mier, and F.C. Hotaling. The demand for Winton cars was so great that dealers could not supply them fast enough.

GABRIEL MOULIN, who took most of the pictures in this book, was one of the best known commercial photographers in San Francisco between 1885 and 1946. In fact, a case could be made that he was one of the true pioneers of modern photography on the Pacific West Coast. Moulin's photographs of the city he loved and of her working people have that peculiar flavor of real life that is the foundation of true documentary art. Virtually all his photographs possess an immense graphic appeal and tend to fit easily into modern photographic aesthetics. As one turns page after page of his photos, one senses that each picture appears to be timeless, although historical, casual, yet accomplished. His images, reminiscent in style and content of some of the work of such geniuses as Paul Martin, Ansel Adams, Imogene Cunningham, Eugene Atget, Alfred Stieglitz, Jacob Riis, and many of the other early classic photojournalists, are important both in helping to define photography as a distinct art and in recording for posterity aspects of a California that once was and will never be again.

This small collection of over 100 prize photographs selected from perhaps 50,000 negatives in the Moulin Studios in San Francisco form a miniature museum of the early motoring times in both the photographic and the real world. In every sense, Gabriel Moulin was an artisan whose craftsman's instinct and ability earn him a niche along side the greatest photographers America ever produced.

Gabriel Moulin
and his touring car.

THE eager motorist in San Francisco with adventure on his mind would start many trips aboard one of the many ferries that traversed the Bay. With nine routes and twenty-nine boats, the frequency of service was very convenient.

There were many regular touring routes that beckoned the motorist. The pages of Duffy's Magazine were filled with stories of motor tours and fascinating places to visit.

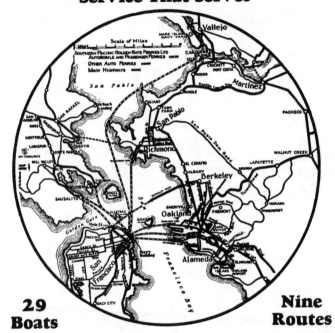

Motorists waiting their turn to board one of the many ferries to Marin County or the East Bay.

One of the most popular tours each Spring was blossom time in the orchards of Santa Clara County

Touring Around the Bay

Of the innumerable short tours open to the San Franciscan with a day's ramble in mind and a motor car at his command, none offers more attractions of a widely diversified nature than the spin about the southern arm of the world-famous bay. Through cities containing half of the population of the state, up one of its most noted peaks, past some of its fairest gardens and farms, the car rolls over more than a hundred miles of floor-like roads.

Starting over Nineteenth avenue from the park, the car is soon spinning over the Sloat boulevard where thirty miles an hour is an easy gait, unaccompanied by the risks that go with it on ordinary roads. Once clear of the city suburbs, the open road leads on through tree-shaded ways, past Burlingame, San Mateo, Belmont and San Carlos, the out-of-doors playground of the well-to-do residents of San Francisco who can afford country places in this garden spot; past Redwood Cty, the county seat of San Mateo, and so over the line into Santa Clara County. Fair Oaks and Menlo Park flash by and the car is gliding through the beautiful campus of Stanford University, over an especially built boulevard recently opened to automobiles.

From the university the car sweeps along southward, through the orchard lands of the Santa Clara Valley, through Santa Clara itself, where the old Spanish mission buildings harbor the students of Santa Clara College, and

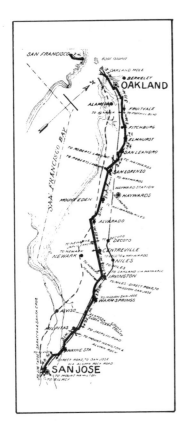

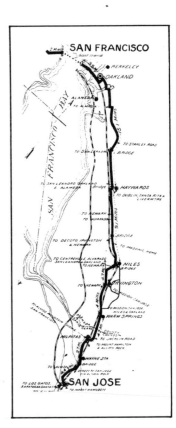

over the broad Alameda into San Jose, where the southern flight is ended.

Turning eastward, toward the long range, a short trip over the valley floor brings the car to Smith Creek, where the ascent of Mount Hamilton begins. Up several thousand feet the car toils, over winding, well-laid-out grades, free from dangerous turns, to Lick Observatory.

Regaining the valley floor, the homeward road is reached at Milpitas and the car headed northward toward Oakland over one of the finest automobile roads in the west. Just out of Niles the car begins to dip over the first rise of the hill boulevard which winds through the foothills of the range rimming the eastern wall of the valley. Above the rolling, smooth surfaces of the hills, where the colors come and go with the changing lights, and far away below, the drowsing waters of the bay sending back the sun rays, the setting is perfect for the peaceful valley near at hand.

MAP. NO. 1
San Francisco to San Jose
via Oakland
San Leandro-Centreville Route
Distance 47.6 miles

MAP NO. 2
San Francisco
to San Jose
Distance 53.2 miles

24

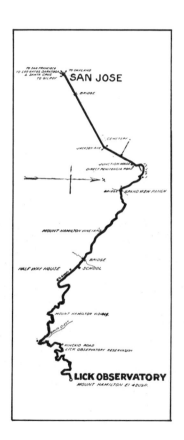

MAP NO. 3
San Jose to
Mount Hamilton
and Lick Observatory
Distance 25.4 miles

Through the thriving little town of Haywards and back into the hills again, the boulevard drops the car so gently into the suburbs of Oakland that the motorist awakens to the fact that he is again in a big city, with somewhat of a start. A short spin through the wide, smooth streets and out over the mole, and the car glides aboard the ferryboat to be landed within twenty minutes at the point where the trip began in the morning.

Reprinted from *Duffy's Magazine*, 1911.

A 1915 Kissel Kar on the golf links at Mount Diablo Estate.

A 1912 Chalmers at an East Bay outing.

On the approach to Mt. Hamilton.

The road to Mt. Hamilton became a greater challenge in the winter.

After a run into Big Basin, in the heart of the Santa Cruz Mountains, a weary party heads for home in their 1919 Reo.

Touring Del Monte

ALL that makes California the Mecca of the scenic loving traveler is comprehended in the tour to Del Monte. Sea, valley and mountain offer a setting under skies that are incomparable, and even the history lover will find remains of the past that more than make the trip worth while, for he will travel El Camino Real, the highway of the priests and soldiers of Spain when that country was mistress of the western world.

No matter how many times this trip is made the motorist will find new delights on each occasion, but to gain even a general idea of its charm he must devote at least three days to the tour. It is hardly necessary to describe the first stage of the journey except to say that it is made by way of San Jose and Gilroy. After Gilroy, the first point of interest is the historic town of San Juan, the seat of one of the earliest Spanish missions and presidios.

Just out of San Juan the famous San Juan grade, at once the terror and delight of the touring autoist, is encountered. After the tortuous ascent is made a glorious view is unfolded from the summit.

Through the Salinas Valley a number of routes lead to the various coast towns which the motorist will want to visit, with Del Monte as the final objective.

After a night spent at Del Monte the town of old Monterey and the Seventeen Mile Drive will draw the atten-

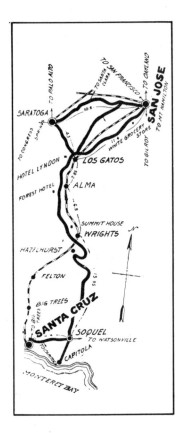

tion of the traveler. Over a road so perfect that it makes the veteran tourist, who has become inured to the average California highway, believe that he is traveling in a dream, the famous drive is traversed. Not much traveling will be done about Monterey and Carmel, as the deep sand does not add to its pleasure, but the motorist will want to spend some time in these places on account of their artistic and historic attractions.

Not desiring to retrace his steps, the traveler has the choice of returning home by way of the Pajaro Valley, Santa Cruz and the Big Tree Basin. Through the Pajaro Valley, by Watsonville, in the spring time the apple orchards in full blossom form a picture as exquisite as the far-famed cherry blossom districts of Japan.

MAP NO. 4
San Jose to Santa Cruz
Distance 39.15 miles
San Jose to Saratoga and Los Gatos
Distance 15.1 miles

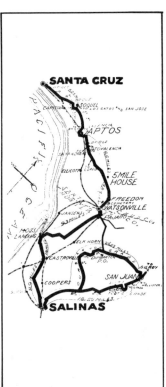

MAP NO. 5
Santa Cruz to Watsonville
Distance 19.2 miles
Watsonville to Salinas
Distance 21 miles
San Juan to Salinas
Distance 16.55 miles
via Dumbarton Road around
San Juan Grade
Distance 20.55 miles

During the summer season Santa Cruz offers many attractions; but probably the greatest of these to the automobilist is the side trip to the Big Tree Basin. The wide canyon, where the big trees grow, is as level as a floor and the state road, within the boundaries of the park, is a credit to its builders. An automobile can be driven within a few hundred feet of the largest tree of the reserve, and the motorist who does not make the trip will lose an opportunity to see California's most famous natural feature without the fatigue involved in trips to more remote and inaccessible groves.

The homeward trip is continued from here over the mountain by way of Los Gatos, thence to San Jose over the usual San Francisco road, bringing to an end one of the most fascinating of the many charming tours offered by this state.

Reprinted from *Duffy's Magazine,* 1911.

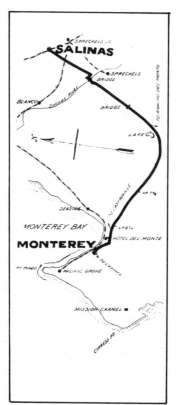

☞
MAP NO. 6
Salinas to Monterey
Distance 20 miles

Ocean Avenue, the main street in the charming town of Carmel.

*A touring coach on the San Juan Grade
headed for Del Monte Lodge at Pebble
Beach near Carmel.*

The resort town of Monte Rio on the Russian River.

Touring Lake County

TAKING the earliest boat for Sausalito, the motorist begins the trip to Lake County while the dew is still on the grass, for night will have fallen before he reaches the end of his first day's journey. Until Petaluma is reached bad roads will be encountered; but the scenery along the way will amply compensate for the discomforts of rough going.

Petaluma marks the gateway of one of California's fairest valleys. Dotted with orchards and vineyards and marked with the most picturesque ranch houses, every turn is a delight to the lover of rural beauty. Every few miles a town greets the eye, and the pleasure-seeking devotee of the touring car will find refreshment for himself and gasoline for the machine. The party that is not out for a record will find it convenient to lunch at McCray's, a delightfully situated old inn, on the bank of the Russian River. Or if one is seeking pleasure, a short ride to the famous resort town of Monte Rio is easily possible.

After this the first mountainous going is encountered, the way winding through the Russian River Canyon, over a narrow and dangerous road which impresses upon the motorist the necessity of good brakes.

At Pieta a turn to the right is made and the car is on the Toll Road grade, one of the finest bits of mountain road in the state. At the Toll House, with the din of the city still echoing in their ears, the party looks down upon Lake

County, almost as remote and fully as picturesque as the highlands of Scotland. From the summit, valley, lake and mountains spread away to the eastward, forming a scenic panorama the sight of which is well worth the fatigues of the journey.

At the end of the Toll Road, lying at the head of Big Valley, Highland Springs is the first of many charming summer resorts which mark the road of the automobilist throughout Lake County. Here the party is afforded its first opportunity to remove the stains of travel in a swimming tank supplied by a living stream of mineral water.

Mt. St. Helena, north of San Francisco.

Lakeport, situated on Clear Lake, is the next point reached after a run over eight miles of valley road, the longest stretch of level going in the county. Here the party that wishes to enjoy its trip to the utmost will stop for a launch ride on the lake.

From Lakeport short trips can be taken to Blue Lakes and Laurel Dell, situated on the shores of two beautiful little lakes, fifteen miles northwest of the town. Another resort in this region which is worth visiting is Witter Springs, over the summit from Laurel Dell.

The party that does not wish to retrace its course can come home either by way of Ukiah, or through the southeastern portion of Lake County over Mount St. Helena and down the Napa Valley to Vallejo.

Reprinted from *Duffy's Magazine*, 1911.

Picnic places abound not only along this addition to Lake County's system of scenic motor routes, but in all parts of the county.

The Napa valley also
offered a wealth of prolific
olive orchards. October was
generally picking time.

The majestic beauty of mountain and lake
are combined in countless panoramas along
the new motor route around Clear Lake.

An early motorist pauses to enjoy the breathtaking view after a long climb.

Touring Lake Tahoe

IN the past only the most venturesome automobilist has dared to drive his car high up into the fastnesses of the Sierras that conceal Lake Tahoe, that most perfect gem among mountain lakes. But with the building of a new road from Sacramento to Tallac, this region promises to become as well known to the touring motorist as any part of the state where the motor car has flourished for the past decade.

The roads about the lake itself are steep and rocky; but this part of the journey has not been the only stretch that has repelled the automobile, for the highways, even in the vicinity of Sacramento, have been nothing to boast of in the past. Recently, however, Sacramento has become an enthusiastic automobile town and the natural result has been a general cry for better roads. The practical outcome has been a fine highway between the Capitol City and Lake Tahoe.

This road will pass through the scarred foothills, where the pioneers took out the gold that made California a state, and into the high mountains which are still as wild as in the days of '49.

The first stage of the journey leads from San Francisco to Sacramento by way of Stockton. The route to Stockton is the same as that followed in the Yosemite Valley tour. From Stockton the northern road through Lodi, Florin and Elk Grove leads to Sacramento.

After leaving Sacramento the Placerville Road, skirting

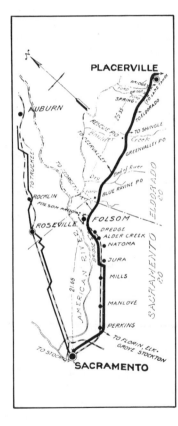

the State Prison at Folsom, is the present route. Placerville, the original Hangtown which gained its name through one of the first summary acts of justice performed by the early Californians, is beautifully situated at the foot of the towering Sierras. During this day's travel the autoist will be reminded on every hand of the stirring days of gold. The gold seeker has left heavy scars to mark his progress and there is hardly a hillside without a tunnel, or a level place without its prospect shaft.

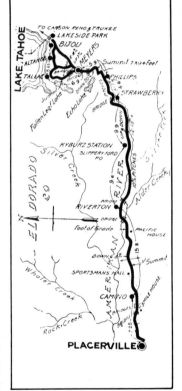

MAP NO. 7
Sacramento to
Placerville
Distance 47.0 miles

MAP NO. 8
Placerville to
Lake Tahoe
Distance 59.5 miles

An early road around the shore of Lake Tahoe.

With a motor car in the
family, picnickers and
Sunday painters were able
to take weekend excursions
not possible in horse-and-
buggy days.

After Placerville is passed it is not long before the steep grade of the Sierras begins. For a time, before the timber belt is reached, the way will be found hot and dusty. Once beneath the shade of the pines, however, the motorist will think himself transported to another clime. Here he will also find the banks beside the roads covered with a coating of thick dust; but if he will remove the coating he will find a bank of snow beneath in many places. When flowers have ceased to bloom on the lower levels, the most gorgeous wild blossoms can be plucked beside the road.

Summit is gained after a climb which makes the autoist either proud of his car or determined to buy a new one with more power, and the final lap of the journey to Tallac, on the lake shore, is commenced.

The automobilist will find the territory in which he can tour about the lake extremely limited, and he will look well to his brakes before he attempts any touring at all. This is more and more made up to him, however, by the beauties of the lake itself and the many ways of amusement it provides. Fishing excursions, bathing and launch trips are the order of the day, pleasant variations of the hours spent in the car.

Reprinted from *Duffy's Magazine*, 1911.

A party of motorists after reaching their destination.

Approaching the grandeur of Yosemite Valley on an early road.

Touring Yosemite Valley

THE usual route selected by the motorist lies through Stockton and Merced; but there are a number of good roads which can be taken through the San Joaquin Valley. Stockton is reached by way of Oakland, Haywards, Livermore and Tracy.

From the bustling metropolis of the San Joaquin a level road sweeps away to Modesto. Here the Turlock road is taken through a country formerly almost as desolate as a desert; but now green and blossoming, watered from the giant La Grange dam, which forms the largest artificial waterfall in the world.

Merced is reached at nightfall by the motorist who is touring for pleasure alone. It is only a hundred and forty miles from San Francisco to Merced; but the autoist who averages more than fifteen or twenty miles an hour over the interior roads of this state does not gain much enjoyment from his ride. Ten hours in a car makes a long day, even over the best of roads, and the motorist will do well to gain a good night's rest at Merced before undertaking the final lap of his journey.

Much of the eighty miles from Merced to El Portal is made through the princely domain of Miller & Lux, the cattle kings of the San Joaquin. At El Portal facilities are provided for the care of the car while the passengers are enjoying the scenery of the valley.

Lights and shadows in the Mariposa Grove of Big Trees in Yosemite National Park. Here Giant Sequoias shoot up 150 feet or more before a branch disturbs their symmetry.

The country about El Portal may tempt the motorist to make side trips before his return; but he will find the roads so steep and rocky that he will not gain much pleasure from these tours unless he is of an adventuresome disposition and well able to stand the tire bill.

Of the wonders of the valley itself it is, perhaps, unnecessary to speak here. Even were this the desire it is improbable that the reader could gain much from this brief article. Yosemite is so utterly beyond adequate description except at the hands of a master, that the present writer shirks the task because of inability. See it, and judge for yourself. It is all that makes the trip worth taking, yet it is a trip no touring motorist should neglect, so great is the reward obtained when one stands on Inspriation Point and sees the valley before him.

Reprinted from *Duffy's Magazine*, 1911.

Tourists in Yosemite view
North America's highest falls
from their Packard roadster.

Winter at the entrance to Yosemite Valley. These visitors will have to go higher to find good skiing conditions.

Summer at the entrance to Yosemite Valley. a perfect spot for a picnic after a long drive.

The Moulin touring car below famous Half Dome.

After a long, hard climb, a spectacular vista.

Just north of Yosemite, Sonora Pass offered motorists another challenge.

High Sierran grandeur north of Yosemite on Ebbetts Pass.

n alpine lake
ong Ebbetts Pass.

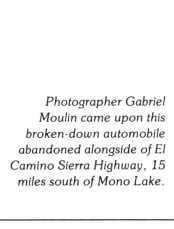

*Photographer Gabriel
Moulin came upon this
broken-down automobile
abandoned alongside of El
Camino Sierra Highway, 15
miles south of Mono Lake.*

Approaching the mountains in Humboldt County.

ONE of the finest trips in California for the automobilist who enjoys mountain traveling is the trip from San Francisco to Crescent City along the coast. Starting from Sausalito or Tiburon the road runs through San Rafael, Petaluma, Santa Rosa, to Ukiah, a distance of about 112 miles. This is the same road that you take in going into Lake County except that you keep straight on instead of turning to the right at Pieta. Continuing straight on through Ukiah, the road turns to the left after about three miles and then commences the first climb of the trip.

Willits is about seventeen miles from Ukiah and the road is fairly steep in places, though in good condition. There is an excellent hotel at Willits and by taking an early start from San Francisco there should be no difficulty in making this run in one day.

From Willits the road continues north through Sherwood, Cummings, Bell Springs, Harris, Camp Five, Rio Dell to Eureka. The distance from Willits to Eureka is about 160 miles and is more than the average motorist would care to do in one day. The stop for the night could be made either at Bell Springs or at Cummings.

While the grades are rather steep in places, attaining at one place an altitude of over 5,000 feet, the roads are in excellent condition and the tourist would have no difficulty at all if he had a car of sufficient horsepower.

Touring the Northern Coast

Alongside a wild river in Humboldt County.

On this portion of the trip every variety of scenery is offered to the motorist; the rivers, mountains, valleys and heavy timber. The run down the Eel River is exceptionally beautiful. From Eureka the road continues on through Arcada, Trinidad, Requa to Crescent City, a distance of 100 miles. On this portion of the trip the road runs most of the way along the cliffs from 500 to 1,000 feet above the ocean, taking occasional turns inland through heavy redwood forests.

For a mountainous county road this is one of the best roads I have ever seen.

The traveler should be careful to time his arrival at the Klamath River at high tide, as the ferry which takes him across cannot reach the banks at low tide.

The last five miles of this stretch, into Crescent City, is made over a hard packed beach where any speed can be made. From Crescent City the motorist will either have to turn back to Eureka or continue over the mountains to Grant's Pass, where he meets the railroad and the main county road to Portland.

Reprinted from *Duffy's Magazine,* 1911.

Smith's Redwood Grove north of Crescent City.

The Avenue of the Giants

*The majesty of the
Redwood forest humbles
the man and his motorcar.*

The Eureka Inn, still a favorite for travelers along the north coast.

A tree large enough to drive a car through.

The tallest trees in the world grow in these North Coast groves.

The Redwood Giants dwarf
the passing motorcar.

Driving inland from the
coastal Redwood groves, a
motorist in Northern
California pauses to gaze at
Mt. Shasta, crowned with
snow the year around.

A dirt road winds its way down the undeveloped Oakland hills.

Touring Oakland and the East Bay Cities

THERE is in Oakland a very large variety of scene which delights the eye and invites attention while it charms the artistic sense. Across the bay rises the massive form of Mount Tamalpais, the summit of which is one of the viewpoints of California, the Golden Gate, and San Francisco.

Between these and Oakland the magnificent stretch of the Bay of San Francisco, an inland sea on which might float the navies of the world.

Back of Oakland rise the Contra Costa range of mountains, buttressed by undulating foothills, from which a level plain slopes to the bay shore.

Located in the very heart of the city is a beautiful lake, 160 acres in area. This inlet from the estuary of San Antonio, an arm of San Francisco Bay, is now separated from tidewater by a broad causeway, so that it is completely landlocked. It affords an ideal sheet of water for rowing and sailing. It is bordered by Lakeside Park and the shore line on the east, and on the northwest is skirted by a broad boulevard.

Radiating from the lake in a central axis are beautiful drives, extending in all directions over smooth thoroughfares for all forms of conveyance, to the foothills and the valleys beyond. A scenic boulevard along the first shelf of the hills affords a ride which is worth coming many miles to enjoy, and one which has become renowned to travelers who have taken this trip out from Oakland.

The sojourner and the seeker for recreation in Oakland will find many points of interest well worth attention, sufficient to employ the time of the visitors for days, so that any one who contemplates a trip to California should not fail to include Oakland in his or her itinerary.

It has been too often the custom of those making the Pacific Coast tour to allow but a few hours' time to Oakland, regarding this city as a pleasant side trip from San Francisco, but today Oakland claims attention as an objective point, as a city that has a separate identity, a city that has a character of its own, that affords abundant attractions to entertain and interest a visitor during an extended stay.

Among the points of special interest to the traveler, the visitor, the tourist, and the sojourner is the Greek Theater at the University of California, which is the most extensive and distinctive structure of its kind in America. Here the California climate lends itself to out-of-door entertainment, and many of the most famous dramatic artists and singers of the world appear. Every pleasant Sunday afternoon during the sessions of the university high-class artists appear under university auspices.

The University of California, one of the greatest educational institutions of the country, is now being trans-

*Far left. Oakland's City Hall.
Near left. Broadway, the
main street in the heart of
Oakland.*

formed along the lines of the Hearst architectural plans by the erection of beautiful buildings, and with its museum, library, and art gallery, is well worth seeing.

From the university at Berkeley another scenic boulevard known as the "tunnel road," leads past Claremont and Lake Chabot into Contra Costa County, which contains some of the most beautiful and sheltered valleys of the state. From here lead roads or trails that reach the redwoods, Grizzly Peak, Mt. Diablo, and other points of interest.

Another charming nearby show place is Piedmont Park, a natural canyon and amphitheater in the foothills beautified with a variety of tropical foliage. Here are located an extensive gallery containing some of the finest pictures of the Pacific Coast, Japanese tea garden, cafe, sulphur springs, and other features.

Trestle Glen, a picturesque retreat with streams and running water, is a pretty spot near Oakland.

Then there is Rock Ridge Park, when many beautiful homes are being built as a result of the view and neighborhood advantages.

The Campanile rises above the campus of the University of California in Berkeley.

The famous Claremont Hotel, high in the East Bay Hills

Claremont, with its magnificent hotel in prospect, is a section which has succeeded to the prestige which formerly belonged to the Nob Hill section of San Francisco.

Leona Heights, up in the foothills, are accessible by rail and afford an ideal viewpoint.

In this vicinity, reached by the road from Dimond Canyon, is the habitat of Joaquin Miller on "The Heights," the mecca of many literary pilgrims.

There are beautiful suburban trips by trolley, local train, or automobile to San Leandro, San Lorenzo, Hayward, and

Newark, broad stretches of fertile fields, orchards, and gardens on either side toward Mission San Jose, replete with historic association and interest; also "Palmdale," with its profuse tropical foliage, its olive trees, its pear trees planted from stock brought over from Spain by the Mission fathers.

Nearby is Mills College, with its park-like surroundings, famous as the Vassar of the Pacific Coast.

Across the estuary and connected with Oakland by excellent car service, is Alameda, the embowered town, retaining extensive areas of live oaks, with its famous bathing beaches, the best on the Pacific Coast.

As one passes across the estuary, there are to be seen forests of masts from ships coming from all parts of the Pacific Coast. Here the fleet of the Alaska Packing Company rendezvous and prepares for return trips to the Arctic.

It has well been said that there is no city in the United States from which one may journey forth on short excursions to a greater change and charm of scenic environment than from Oakland, California.

These are but a few of the attractions, coupled with a genial and invigorating climate which ought to impress upon the tourist the fact that Oakland should be given a prominent place on the itinerary of the California trip.

Reprinted from *Motorland*, courtesy California State
Automobile Association

*Traveling beneath the estuary between
Oakland and Alameda in the "Tube."*

Sunday drivers crowd a road in Golden Gate Park.

Touring San Francisco

IF California is the Golden State, then San Francisco is the gemstone set in this metallic band. Surrounded by the emerald and sapphire Bay it glistens in the sun like a setting for the *Arabian Nights*. The island-like site at the tip of a peninsula helps create the unique atmosphere of the City: a thriving fishing industry, ocean-going commerce, and an international population.

The best view for the newcomer is had from the crest of Twin Peaks, a remarkable pair of hills standing next to each other south of the downtown area. The road to the crest is one of the more challenging found in San Francisco, itself a city built on hills. The vista that greets the intrepid motorist makes the effort worthwhile: To the west is the broad expanse of blue ocean, often with its white fog chilling the breezes; to the east is the Bay, stretching south to San Jose, and the East Bay cities surrounding Oakland, and further beyond the massive cone of Mt. Diablo; to the south the peninsula carries the infamous San Andreas fault between two ridges; and the City sparkles to the north.

Landmarks easily identifiable from the Twin Peaks summit are St. Ignatius church with its twin spires rising from the University of San Francisco's hilltop, the Golden Gate with Mt. Tamalpais beyond in Marin County, the Cliff House at the northwestern corner; Nob, Russian, and Telegraph Hills; the Ferry Building at the end of Market Street

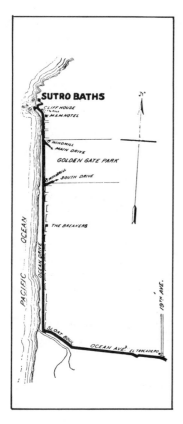

with the piers extending north and south on the waterfront. From Twin Peaks El Camino Real, U.S. 101, lies just to the east, giving easy access to the City's civic center, dominated by the magnificent City Hall crowned with its golden dome. Nearby is the "Wall Street of the West"—Montgomery Street; crossing Montgomery is California Street whose cable cars carry tourists and residents alike to the top of Nob Hill, graced by the magnificent Grace Cathedral and the City's two great hotels, the Fairmont and the Mark Hopkins. Due north lie the cuisinary delights of Fisherman's Wharf, but on the way are the not-to-be-missed sights of Grant Avenue and Chinatown.

West of the Wharf area is the Palace of Fine Arts, a remnant from the Pan-Pacific exposition of 1915, and one of the world's most beautiful military installations, the Presidio. Continuing through the beautiful cypress-shaded grounds takes us to the exclusive residential area of Sea Cliff and, further, to Lincoln Park and its golf course which over-looks the straits of the Golden Gate and surrounds the

☞
MAP NO. 9
Ocean Drive and
Sloat Boulevard,
San Francisco

☞
MAP NO. 10
South Drive through
Golden Gate Park,
San Francisco

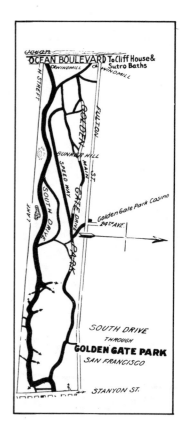

Palace of the Legion of Honor. Eastward to the ocean shore, the Cliff House stands majestically above the surf. Below is Sutro Baths with its warm salt water pools and the rugged Seal Rocks with their lively animal population.

Ocean Beach falls away southward below the Cliff House, Playland's amusement park immediately below to landward and Golden Gate Park just beyond. The huge park, built on rolling sand dunes, contains museums, bandshells, flower gardens, play areas, and a network of roads and paths making everything optimally accessible. A few miles south of the park, just on the Pacific is the San Francisco Zoo and the largest salt water pool in the world, Fleishhacker.

Whatever your interest, you will find something to satisfy it in San Francisco. Its colorful background and rich, individual character have never become mere history. The City is as thrilling today as it was when the first loud cry of "Gold" drew people to it from around the world. San Francisco. . . the City that was never a village!

MAP NO. 11
Presidio Reservation,
San Francisco

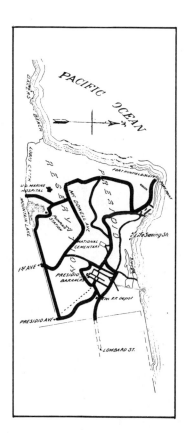

A Sunday excursion could include a stroll by the ocean below Cliff House.

The exclusive Sea Cliff district, before the Golden Gate Bridge was built.

If your car could make the climb,
the view from Twin Peaks was marvelous.

On the winding road down from Twin Peaks.

Before the advent of the motel, hotels accommodated the needs of motorists as best they could.

The elegant side entrance of the famous Palace Hotel

A popular destination for motorists in 1915—the Pan-Pacific Exposition.

Early speeders came to San Francisco's old
Hall of Justice to pay their fines.

*A ride on solid-rubber tires over
cobblestones made for a heady keg of beer.*

Telling How Automobile Enthusiasts May Enjoy, Any Time of the Year, the Picturesque Run Between Los Angeles and San Francisco

Coast Country Motoring

THE map accompanying this short article shows the topographical conditions of the road from San Francisco to Los Angeles, and it is to be recommended to automobilists as trustworthy in every respect. While there are no guide-posts in position between these two cities, still there will be but little trouble in following this map, especially if the tourists take occasion once in a while en route to inquire the road directions from residents. They may be a trifle mixed upon distances, but that is the strong feature of this map. Those travelers, who have had occasion to rely upon the information as to distances to "the next town," have little faith in a native's declarations, and this new routing will eliminate such necessity.

Motor-car touring has received an added stimulus in the passing of the new California state law covering the operation of automobiles upon the public highway, since the roadways hitherto closed, in some counties, are now fully opened, but it will be well to remember that such roadways are and always have been, dangerous for horses meeting machines upon the grades, and this map, in consequence, does not show the road between Los Olivos and Santa Barbara over the San Marcos pass. Several accidents have occurred there, and it would be well for auto-tourists to take the longer and harder trip via Gaviota than to incur the danger of accidents and resultant damage suits.

Among the points upon this map that attention should be called to especially are the possibility of taking a road via Alvarado to Centerville, and thence to San Jose, upon the Oakland side of San Francisco bay as a break from the regular Hayward-Decoto run. At San Jose continue out the main street, upon which the Vendome and St. James hotels are located, in order to be certain that you strike the Gilroy road. In Gilroy, follow right along the main street, keeping to that road until San Juan is reached, by way of Sargent's. Upon reaching the mission town, run by the Plaza hotel, opposite the Mission, and then turn at right angles for two squares, then one to the left, and the road running to your right is the one that leads to the base of the San Juan grade, that old-time *bete noir* of the auto of little power.

Coasting down the other side of the San Juan, run along until you reach two roads forking at a bridge. Take the one to the right that crosses the small waterway, and then continue on your left—unless you care to stop over at restful Del Monte—into the town of Salinas. There you also run along the main street, turning to your left at the Jeffries

house, continue for two squares, and then, turning to the right, the motor car will be on the direct road to Kings City. Do not, under any circumstances, go into that town over the sand-strewn bridge, unless you need gasoline, but keep on the road to the right and run over the grade into Jolon.

After leaving this latter place, avoid Pleyto, taking the only other road to Bradley. Then take the Indian valley run, instead of fording the two intervening rivers between Bradley and San Miguel. Keep upon the side of the river that the Indian valley road brings you after you circle the school house until you are directly opposite San Miguel, where you will find a bridge crossing the river. At Paso Robles you will enjoy the hot springs and a good rest.

There is little else to remember until you leave Santa Maria, when the Foxen canon road presents better facilities in reaching Los Olivos than any other route. Your run then takes you preferably into Gaviota and then to Santa Barbara. Gasoline can be obtained all along the way, but it will be well to fill your tanks at the larger towns.

By Wallace Everett, reprinted courtesy Lane Publishing,
Sunset, May, 1911.

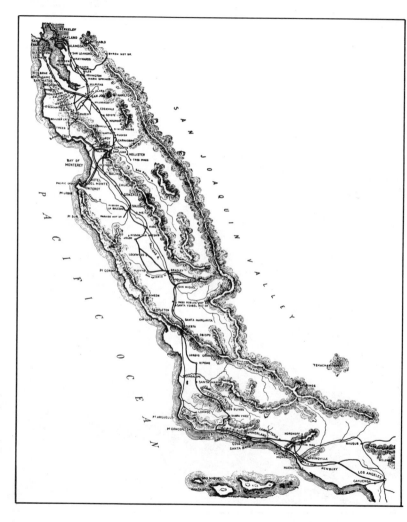

MAP NO. 12
The way to travel by automobile between San Francisco and Los Angeles—based on notes and records made by the writer of the accompanying article, who went over this route especially in the interest of *Sunset Magazine*

California's earliest "industry" was gold. By 1910 it was oil. Here, in Venice, California, derricks as thick as trees greet the motorist.

Touring about Los Angeles

HEN we first left the confines of the city we steered straight for the sunset; the wayfarer from the far inland states always longs for a glimpse of the ocean and it is usually his first objective. The road, smooth and hard as polished slate, runs for a dozen miles between green fields, with here and there a fringe of palms or eucalyptus trees and showing in many places the encroachments of rapidly growing suburbs. So seductively perfect is the road that the twenty miles slip away almost before we are aware; we find ourselves crossing the canal in Venice and are soon surrounded by the wilderness of "attractions" of this famous resort.

There is little to remind us of its Italian namesake save the wide stretch of sea that breaks into view and an occasional gondola on the tiny canal; in the main it is far more suggestive of Coney Island than of the Queen of the Adriatic.

On gala days it is interesting to differentiate the types that pass before one, from the countryman from the inland states, "doing" California and getting his first glimpse of a metropolitan resort, to the fast young sport from the city, to whom all things have grown common and blase and who has motored down to Venice because he happened to have nowhere else to go. Venice seems to be one of the favorite haunts of the latter class and their drunken joy-rides have resulted in many wrecks on the fine highways leading to the city. On our first trip we passed a badly disabled car by the roadside and saw several others at various times later. Most of this sorry business occurs in the small hours of the night, making it exceedingly difficult for the police to deal with. In case of one wreck, for instance, in which several were injured and a large car was burned, the parties were spirited away before the officers reached the scene of the disaster, to keep their names from the public. Unfortunately, Venice, like so many other beautiful places near Los Angeles, has been marred by the proliferation of oil derricks.

We found little to interest us in the California Venice, save odd specimens of humanity, thus we usually slipped into the narrow "Speedway" connecting the town with Ocean Park and Santa Monica. Why they call it the Speedway I am at a loss to know, for it is barely a dozen feet wide in places and intersected with alleys and streets every few feet, so that the limit of fifteen miles is really dangerously high. The perfect pavement, however, made it the most comfortable route—though there may be better now—and it also takes one through the liveliest part of Ocean Park, another resort very much like Venice and almost continuous with it. These places are full of hotels and lodging-houses, mostly of the less pretentious and inexpensive class, and they are filled during the winter season mainly by Eastern tourists. In the summer the immense bathing beaches attract crowds from the city. The Pacific Electric brings its daily contingent of tourists and the streets are constantly crowded with motors—sometimes hundreds of them. All of which contribute to the animation of the scene in these popular resorts.

In Santa Monica we found quite a different atmosphere. It is situated on an eminence overlooking the Pacific and to the north lie the blue ranges of the Santa Monica Mountains, visible from every part of town. Ocean Drive, a broad boulevard, skirts the edge of the promontory, screened in places by rows of palms, through which flashes the blue expanse of the sea. At its northern extremity the drive drops down a sharp grade to the floor of the canyon, which opens on a wide, sandy beach—one of the cleanest and quietest to be found so near Los Angeles.

This canyon, with its huge sycamores and clear creek brawling over the smooth stones, had long been an ideal resort for picnic parties, but in the course of a single year we found it much changed. The hillside had been terraced and laid out with drives and here and there a summer house had sprung up, fresh with paint or stucco. The floor of the valley

Santa Monica Pier and Pacific Coast Highway.

was also platted and much of the wild-wood effect already gone. All this was the result of a great "boom" in Santa Monica property, largely the work of real estate promoters. Other additions were being planned to the eastward and all signs pointed to rapid growth of the town. It already has many fine residences and cozy bungalows embowered in flowers and shrubbery, among which roses, geraniums and palms of different varieties predominate.

Leaving the town, we usually followed the highway leading through the grounds of the National Soldiers' Home.

From there one may follow Wilshire Boulevard, which enters the most pretentious section of the city, surrounding the beautiful little West Lake Park; or he may turn into Sunset Boulevard and pass through Hollywood. A short distance from the Soldiers' Home is Beverly Hills, with its immense hotel—a new resort town where many Los Angeles citizens have summer residences. A vast deal of work has been done by the promoters of the town; the well-paved streets are bordered with roses, geraniums, and rows of palm trees, all skillfully arranged by the landscape-gardener. It is a pretty place, though it seemed to us that the sea winds swept it rather fiercely during several of the visits we made. Another unpleasant feature was the groups of oil derricks which dot the surrounding country, though these will doubt-

less some time disappear with the exhaustion of the fields. The hotel is a modified mission type, with solid concrete walls and red tile roof, and its surroundings and appointments are up to the famous California standard at such resorts.

Hollywood is now continuous with the city, but it has lost none of that tropical beauty that has long made it famous. Embowered in flowers and palms, with an occasional lemon grove, its cozy and in some cases palatial homes never fail to charm the newcomer. Once it was known as the home of Paul de Longpre, the flower painter, whose Moorish-looking villa was the goal of the tourist and whose gorgeous creations were a never-failing wonder to the rural art critic.

Returning home, we always felt welcome at one of the most magnificent hotels in the country, the Ambassador. Just South of Wilshire Boulevard, its gracious rooms and magnificent decor provided a delightful pause in the day.

If a newcomer, you will want to drive about the town of Pasadena—truly an enchanted city, whose homes revel in never-ending summer. Is there the equal of Orange Grove Avenue in the world? I doubt it. A clean, wide, slate-smooth street, bordered by magnificent residences embowered in flowers and palms and surrounded by velvety green lawns, extends for more than two miles. In a decade the city has grown from a village of nine thousand people to some five

A lone motorist on a palm-flanked boulevard in Beverly Hills.

The Ambassador Hotel was world famous from the day it opened — perhaps because of its parking lot.

times that number and its growth still proceeds by leaps and bounds. It has three famous resort hotels, whose capacity is constantly taxed during the winter season, and there are many magnificent churches and public buildings. One of the most famous is the Green Hotel, a place you must stop and visit. Pasadena's beauty and culture, together with the advantages of the metropolis which elbows it on the west, and the unrivaled climate of California, give to Pasadena first place among the residence towns of the country.

And if one follows the long stretch of Colorado Street to the eastward, it will lead him into Foothill Boulevard, and I doubt if in all California—which is to say in all the world— there is a more beautiful roadway than the half dozen miles between Pasadena and Monrovia. Here the Baldwin Oaks skirt the highway on either side—great century-old Spanish and live oaks, some gnarled and twisted into a thousand fantastic shapes and others the very acme of arboreal symmetry—hundreds of them, hale and green despite their age.

By Thomas Murphy, reprinted from *On Sunset Highways*.

Colorado Boulevard in Pasadena looking west.

*Pasadena's magnificent
Green Hotel*

SOME interesting figures regarding automobile registration are disclosed by a recent census compiled by *Automotive Industries*. There are 7,904,271 motor vehicles in use in the United States, a gain of a million and a half in the past year. There is a car for every 13.52 persons in the country.

Ohio leads in registration, with Pennsylvania, Illinois, New York, California, Iowa, Michigan, Indiana, Texas and Minnesota occupying the first ten places in the order named. Ohio has 567,000 cars, Pennsylvania 506,085, Illinois 497,318, California 421,327, Iowa 405,182, Michigan 351,762, Indiana 302,308, Texas 298,234, Minnesota 295,898. Nevada trails the list with 9,383. The State of Washington is eighteenth with 143,651 and Oregon twenty-seventh with 89,933.

Reprinted from *Motorland*, courtesy California State Automobile Association

The Motor Cars

AVBVRN

Peering under the hood in 1921.

CHANDLER

San Francisco, 1922.

*Chandler. A two-car
garage, 1923.*

*Chandler. With
a youthful version.*

Golden Gate Park

Temperature gauge.

4-door Touring Car, brakes
holding on a steep hill,
San Francisco.

New and used available on
Van Ness Avenue

Lincoln Park, San Francisco

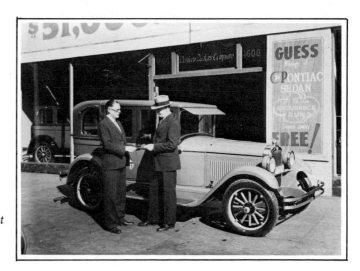

Sold to a new motorist

Rickenbacker
A · CAR · WORTHY · OF · ITS · NAME

Climbing Webster Street Hill,
San Francisco

Roosevelt

Roosevelt '8' in Golden Gate Park

On Van Ness Avenue, San Francisco

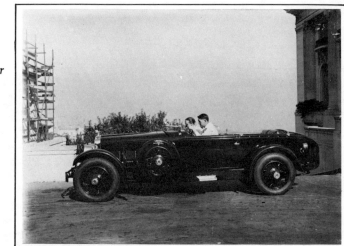

Stutz Roadster

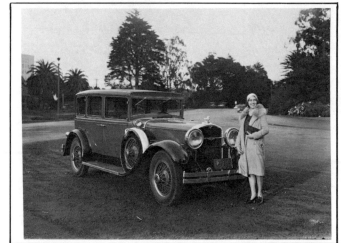

Stutz '8'

Whippet

Whippet '6' in Golden Gate Park

Whippet 2-door sports car

Whippet "Speedster"

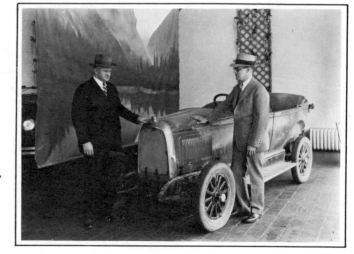

In Golden Gate Park, 1923

A 2-door Willys-Knight

Buick

Gus Anthony in his classic 1904 Buick. Known as one of the foremost auto enthusiasts in the Bay Area, Gus was forever experimenting with fast-flying automobiles of every make and design.

Packard

The showroom for the latest Packard automobiles from Detroit, located on "auto row" on Van Ness Avenue in San Francisco. This building and its interior were designed by famed architect Bernard Maybeck.

The brand new Cadillacs and a new La Salle (left) pause outside the showroom

Here the motorist could acquire tires and rims as well as fuel.

Hints to the Motor Tourist

IF the motorist can afford it he ought never to start off on a long, hard tour without new tires. If this seems too great an extravagance, at least put new casings on the rear wheels. A wise man will have the rims cleaned, sandpapered and painted with aluminum paint forestalling all sticking or rusting. New tires ensure you against a host of bothers, and may add much to the pleasure of the trip. If you feel that your car when loaded for touring is too heavy for the tires—a common fault—get a larger size that will fit the same rims. Tire manufacturers have recently awakened to the need for these extra sizes and advertise them in their catalogues. Another half-inch will give you four or five hundred pounds greater carrying capacity.

There is nothing about an automobile more worth thought and foresight than tires and tire accessories. Get the best pump made—a single action one—no backbreaking "compound." Be sure and take a Michelin "lifter," so that you will not strain your valves in removing punctured inner tubes; have a little store of plungers and caps, as well as one of those handy tools for re-cutting the valve threads, both inside and out; if you use one of the many varieties of "detachables," equip yourself with the spare parts most likely to be needed—especially providing yourself with an extra one of the rings that lock the casing into place. These rings easily "go out of whack" as your chauffeur would say—and when they are "out of whack" they are exasperating things to struggle with.

Personally I prefer ordinary clinchers, with a Stepney wheel by way of reserve. This wheel ought to be employed a great deal more than it is, especially on smaller cars. In trouble it is your best friend, and where women drive, it is absolutely essential. That all taxicab companies use the Stepney speaks for itself. While on the subject let me warn the inexperienced reader against running on flat tires. No matter where a puncture overtakes you, move not an inch till you have installed a new tube or locked on your Stepney. Don't be tempted by a shady nook a hundred feet beyond. A hundred feet can cut your inner tube to ribbons, and injure your casing beyond repair. Let the sun beat down on your defenseless head, let the ground burn your unfortunate feet, let the spot be the worst you could have chosen in the whole state of California—but *stay where you are*. If you don't, you are a tire-murderer and unworthy to own a car. You might as well take your watch and smash it between two stones. Never mind your wife's pleading, but hustle out the jack and get busy. You will be rewarded, not only in the bright hereafter—but *now*.

It is assumed that you take the ordinary complement of tools, though a word might be put in for a big Stillson wrench. These wrenches, in emergencies, are invaluable,

and are not as frequently carried as they should be. Not only are they usually better than the special tools provided for removing the wheels, but in the case of a refractory spark-plug or valve-cap they are indispensable. Of all petty disasters there is none more exasperating than to have a broken spark-plug stick in the threads. It is no good *in*, and it won't come out; you have no wrench large enough to start the valve-cap; happy then is the motorist who has a life-saving Stillson in the bottom of his tool-box. The caps of some radiators, too, are of a round pattern that sometimes defy your fingers to remove them. I have seen people driven to the expedient of knocking a hole through the cap in order to admit water. A big enough Stillson will unloose Mr. Cap in the twinkling of an eye, and if carefully used will not bruise the brass. The largest sizes of these wrenches are to be preferred.

Before beginning a long tour the hose-connections ought to be carefully examined, and if there is any question about them, new ones should be substituted. Always give a hose-connection the benefit of the doubt—rubber is too perishable to trust. To renew them costs hardly anything, and if

The gas station attendant quickly became an important friend to the motorist.

one should crack on the road serious harm may be done to your engine, without counting the inevitable annoyance and delay. It is never a bad plan to carry an eighteen-inch length of hose of the gauge you use. Hose is an irreplaceable article when you are a hundred miles from anywhere.

As for engine spare parts, that is for the individual owner to settle for himself. Many go to both extremes—some burdening themselves with almost a duplicate engine; other unconcerned to take even extra insulated wire. Personally I should be guided by my previous experience with the car—carrying a spare universal joint in case I had ever had one break—a spare crankpin, etc., if I had had trouble here before—ball-races and cones if the wheels had once shown

In 1908, roadside tire repairs were frequently required, and motor cars carried a well-stocked tool kit. Fortunately, fellow motorists believed in lending a helping hand.

signs of weakness. But most of our modern cars are extraordinarily well made, and it may be that the motorist never has had anything "give out." In that event I should be content to take a spare valve, some insulated wire, an intake and an exhaust spring, and perhaps some extra brake-lining. Where a coil is used spare vibrators and set-screws are essential. Iridium points on set-screws are well worth the higher price charged for them.

Talking of induction coils (where there is no supplementary magneto), the beginner should get a mechanic to show him how to cut out the switch, and wire directly to the cross-bar of the coil. Most switches are wretchedly made—you can look through a whole catalogue and not find a good one—and many a poor fellow has been stuck for hours by a faulty switch when a direct wire would have resolved his difficulties in a minute. It is well to remember that wherever there is a telephone, dry batteries are not far distant. The country exchanges, if properly approached, will always help you out.

The beginner, if he has a carburetor with an automatic air inlet of the ordinary type, should likewise get instructed how to screen the aperture with a handkerchief or a bit of cheese-cloth—so as to adjust a new "mixture" in the case of the automatic part going out of business. The carburetor I have in mind is probably used on the half of our American

cars, and is very good indeed. But the company that manufactures it seems to be becoming very slack in its prosperous old age, and its factory inspection every year grows worse. Bad workmanship is overlooked, and hence, as history is apt to repeat itself, the tyro should learn how to use his handkerchief.

I ought to have put down a spare float as one of the essentials to carry. In buying it be sure and get the *right* float for your type of carbureter. The automobile supply man is a careless individual, often unfamiliar with the things he deals in, and he is capable of handing you out a float for a Model D when you want Model K 1909—or you may innocently receive a float for an altogether different brand of carbureter. The careless supply man has a lot to answer for. He sells you metric threads instead of "half-inch standard"; inner tubes that don't fit; grease guns without a plunger. Don't think that he is intentionally a villain; he has exactly what you want on the next shelf; but a tendency to replace articles in the wrong boxes is his prevailing defect. Verify in the shop everything you buy, and thus head off trouble.

A 1910 Rambler (left) and a
1912 Stoddard Dayton (right)
stop at a flourishing auto parts store.

By the way, the present fashion in kerosene lamps is a very bad one. Every lamp ought to have a "bale," as it is called—that is to say a handle to carry it with; and every lamp ought also to be able to stand alone—flat-bottomed and solid, wherever it is put. Most of our lamps have neither bales nor standing-upness. They have to be carried in your arms like a baby, or built about with stones if you wish them to stay upright while mending a puncture in the dark. On tour there is ever a chance you may need your lamps as lanterns, and may have to carry one for miles to some far-off ranch-house. You will then want to swing it on a bale—not hug it to your bosom and scorch your fingers. Not one car in twenty has a lamp worth owning. If you should deem it too extravagant to change your side-lights, at any rate get a tail-light with a handle, and enough of a base to stand comfortably on the ground.

In the line of little conveniences a folding steel foot-rule is certainly worth the twenty-five cents it costs. Garage mechanics are frightful sinners in the way they plunge greasy files or spills of paper or any old thing into the gas-tank to see how much you need. Your steel rule is compact and portable, and you will not feel it in your pocket. Don't allow anything else to be used. If you are an economical man you will learn to gauge your tank exactly, and will thus probably save anything from twenty-five cents to a dollar a day. The gasoline can is an elastic measure and usually errs against you. Leave it to Mr. Croesus to say: "Fill her up." A wise motorist knows how much gas he wants—*and sees that he gets it.*

If you wish to take firearms or fishing-rods—and no prolonged tour in California would be complete without them—get a saddler to make you a sort of giant leather holster that you can strap vertically to the side of the car. In this manner you can carry a loaded rifle or shotgun, muzzle down, with absolute safety, and be able to draw it out in the shake of a lamb's tail. Revolvers are dangerous to have about; if the motorist *must* have one the best place for it is in the pocket on the tonneau door, where it had better be left throughout the tour. Do not let any member of your party go "heeled." A rifle is a thousand times safer than the biggest frontier "gun" or complicated deadly "automatic."

By Lloyd Osbourne, reprinted Courtesy Lane Publishing,
Sunset, May 1911.

There were those embarrassing times when the distraught motorist required some old-fashioned assistance.

And there were other times when everything went *wrong.*

A FEW EXTRACTS FROM THE
SAN FRANCISCO TRAFFIC ORDINANCE.

The following rules are in force in most all cities, and if not, should be. Learn them by heart, and by following them closely we will not have so many kicks from the general public:

Sec. 1. Defines the words "street," "curb," "vehicle" and "moving travel and traffic."

Sec. 2. Provides that vehicles shall always be propelled with due regard for the safety and convenience of the public.

Sec. 3. Provides that vehicles shall travel on the right side of the street and as near the curb as possible.

Sec. 4. Provides for surrendering portion of narrow streets upon meeting other vehicles.

Sec. 5. Provides that in being overtaken by another vehicle the person so overtaken shall give way to the right.

Sec. 6. Provides that slowly moving vehicles shall proceed as closely as possible to the righthand curb, allowing more rapidly moving vehicles to pass to the left.

Sec. 7. Provides that before changing the course of vehicles drivers must first see that there is sufficient space to change such course and give plainly visible or audible sign to others traveling behind.

Sec. 8. Provides that in turning to the right into another street to turn the corner as near the right hand curb as possible.

Sec. 9. Provides that in turning to the left into another street drivers must pass to the right of and beyond the center of street intersection before turning.

Sec. 10. Provides that in crossing from one side of a street to another drivers must do so by turning to the left and so as to head in the same direction as the traffic on that side of the street.

Sec. 11. Provides that vehicles when stopping shall always do so with the right-hand side nearest the curb.

Appendix

Sec. 12. Provides that in stopping vehicles position must be as near curb as possible, except in momentary stops to allow passing of pedestrians or another vehicle.

Sec. 13. Provides that no vehicle shall remain backed up to the curb except when actually being loaded or unloaded.

Sec. 14. Provides that vehicles moving upon certain stated streets shall have right of way over vehicles moving upon intersecting streets.

Sec. 15. Provides that Fire Department, ambulances and U.S. Mail shall have right of way.

Sec. 16. Provides that moving vehicles must keep at least four feet from running board or lowest step of street cars discharging passengers.

Sec. 17. Provides that animals attached to vehicles backed up to the curb shall be turned at right angles to vehicles and in the direction of traffic.

Sec. 18. Provides for gong, bell or horn to be used only when necessary to give warning.

Sec. 19. Provides that no sound producing instrument of a loud or annoying character shall be used, such as "sirens" or similar devices.

Sec. 20. Provides that in leaving vehicles standing on grades wheels shall be thrown in toward the curb.

Sec. 21. Provides that persons operating vehicles shall not willfully interfere with street railway traffic.

Sec. 22. Provides that street cars only shall have right of way on street car tracks.

Sec. 23. Provides that no person shall catch on to or otherwise attach himself to any moving vehicle without proper permission.

Sec. 24. Provides that bicycles shall not travel closely in the wake of other vehicles.

Sec. 25. Provides that motor vehicles shall not visibly emit an unduly great amount of smoke, steam or products of combustion.

Sec. 26. Provides that motor vehicles shall operate in as noiseless a manner as possible with closed "mufflers."

Sec. 27. Provides that no person under 18 years of age shall operate motor vehicles without permission from the Board of Police Commissioners, who may, at their option, grant such permission, provided, however, that such person is not under 16 years of age.

Sec. 28. Provides that animals shall not be "broken" nor dangerous animals be driven upon the streets.

Sec. 29. Provides that the speed be not more than 10 miles per hour upon heavily traveled streets and 15 miles per hour upon other streets, and also names the "heavily traveled" streets.

Sec. 30. Provides for the use of lights on motor vehicles from one-half hour after sunset to one-half hour before sunrise.

Sec. 31. Provides for the use of light on bicycles, motor bicycles, and similar vehicles from one-half hour after sunset to one-half hour before sunrise.

Sec. 32. Provides that the Board of Police Commissioners shall cause copies of this ordinance to be posted in certain stated places.

Sec. 33. Provides penalties for violation of the terms of ordinance.

Sec. 34. Provides for repeal of ordinances in conflict with this ordinance.

Sec. 35. Provides that this ordinance shall take effect 30 days after its passage, which was on January 15, 1909.

In addition to the foregoing, attention is directed to Ordinance No. 902, which empowers and directs police officers to enforce ordinances.

A FEW POINTERS.

Don't try to make fast time. Take it easy and enjoy the country.

Don't forget that "Duffy's Magazine" has all the road maps. Take one along.

Don't give information about an accident to anyone except the police.

Don't let witnesses get away without taking their names and addresses.

If your car is registered in another state, it is not necessary to again register it in California.

Don't drive fast over rough roads. It injures your engine, car and tires, and wears you and your passengers out.

Don't be dissatisfied with the car, or the roads, or the weather, or the hotels. Take things as they come and get the most out of everything.

Don't forget your gasoline. It is better to stop and fill up while you know you have plenty than to run out five miles from any supply.

Don't hurry. Take plenty of time for meals. Start at a comfortable time in the morning and stop for the night before you are tired out.

Don't forget your registration and licenses when starting on a tour. Your own state license may protect you in other states, and it may not.

Don't fail to stop if everything about the car is not going just right. "A stitch in time saves nine." And five minutes by the roadside may save fifty dollars in the shop.

Don't forget that "Duffy's Magazine" Co. have put this excellent publication before you at a price that, when it gets soiled or torn, you can afford to buy a new copy.

Don't carry too many passengers. You will be more comfortable with fewer people and carrying your baggage with you than with so many people that you have to ship it.

Don't forget that a "friend in need" is a copy of "Duffy's Magazine." It will tell you just what you wish to know. Get a copy at any newsdealer or automobile garage or supply house.

Don't let small bits of foreign matter drop into the cylinder when re-

Don't openly disregard speed laws and ordinances. Flagrant violation of them may mean arrest, expense and delay, and is sure to cause prejudice against the automobile. There is a tendency on the part of the public toward a liberal interpretation of speed laws and limits which should be fostered by decency rather than discouraged by abuse.

Don't forget to tell them you "saw it in Duffy's Magazine." Your kindness will be appreciated and rewarded by helping us issue a better magazine than ever. Remember that the price we charge you for this copy is about one-third its actual cost. We can only hope to break even by proving that we are giving results to our patrons.

FERRY REGULATIONS FOR AUTOMOBILES.

Southern Pacific Company. 1. Automobiles must reach the dock at either end of the ferry, so as to be in readiness to board the boat at least five minutes prior to leaving time.

2. Automobiles will not be allowed upon the aprons or gangways leading to the boat, when such aprons or gangways are occupied by passengers, entering or leaving.

3. All lights and fires in automobiles must be extinguished before machines are allowed upon ferryboats, and not again relighted until machines have left the boat.

Machines operated solely by gasoline may use their own power entering and leaving the boat, but when at rest electric current must be turned off and engines kept stationary.

Machines operated by steam will be permitted to go on or off the boats under their own steam—without fires—provided pressure will permit; otherwise, they must be moved on or off by deckhands.

4. Any machines, which, on inspection, show leakage, either of lubricating oil or of gasoline, will not be allowed to board ferryboats until repairs have been made.

moving spark plugs. A particle of porcelain or any other hard substance soon cuts a cylinder so that it has to be removed.

Don't go too far without stopping. A short stop will rest not only you and the passenger, but the engine and tires as well, and the balance of the trip will be all the more enjoyable.

Don't start on a tour without preparation for any and all emergencies. Carry extra tires and parts. Provide against the weather. Carry plenty of tools. Be sure your car is in good shape, and then keep it so.

Don't be inconsiderate of others using the highways. Their appreciation of any little courtesies you may show them, and the satisfaction of knowing that you have made friends rather than enemies for your favorite sport will be among the pleasantest remembrances of your trip.

You cannot keep your old number for your new car. The number goes with the car.

When you sell your machine get a "transfer of ownership" blank from the secretary of the club and send it together with one dollar to the secretary of state, who will issue a license to the new owner.

Don't map out your tour like a railroad time table and try to keep the schedule. Select your objective and lay out the route with reference to roads, hotels, etc. Map out roughly about where you expect to stop, and then make up your mind to go where you please and stop when you feel like it.

Automobiles having canvas aprons must have all surplus oil removed therefrom, and the relief cocks of machines having metal aprons must be closed, before machines board the ferryboats, to avoid dripping of oil on floors of gangways or decks of ferryboats.

5. Automobiles must, while crossing the bay, remain upon the deck in the rear of the enclosed portion of the boat.

6. The blowing of horns by occupants of automobiles, while crossing on ferryboats, is prohibited.

AUTOMOBILE LAW FOR CALIFORNIA.

Defining the Terms Used Herein. Section 1. Subdivision 1. The words and phrases used in this act shall for the purposes of this act, unless the same be contrary to or inconsistent with the context, be construed as follows: (1) "motor vehicle" shall include all vehicles propelled by any power other than muscular power, provided that nothing herein contained shall, except the provisions of subdivisions three, four and five of section three and subdivision one of section four of this act, apply to motor cycles, motor bicycles, traction engines or road rollers; (2) "public highways" shall include any highway, county road, state road, public street, avenue, alley, park, parkway, driveway or public place in any county, or incorporated city and county, city or town; (3) "closely built up" shall mean (a) the territory of any county or incorporated city and county, city or town contiguous to a public highway which is at that point built up with structures devoted to business, (b) the territory of any county or incorporated city and county, city or town contiguous to a public highway not devoted to business, where for not less than one-quarter of a mile the dwelling houses on such highway average less than one hundred feet apart, provided that the local authorities having charge of such highway shall have placed conspicuously thereon at both ends of such closely built up section signs of sufficient size to be easily readable by a person using the highway, bearing the words "Slow down to

_____ miles," inserting in the blank space the number of miles to which the speed is to be reduced, and also an arrow pointing in the direction where the speed is to be reduced; (4) "local authorities" shall include all boards of supervisors, trustees or councils, committees and other public officials of counties, or incorporated cities and counties, cities or towns; (5) "chauffeur" shall mean any person operating a motor vehicle as mechanic, employee or for hire.

Registration of Motor Vehicles. Sec. 2. Subdivision 1. Every owner or person hereafter acquiring a motor vehicle shall, for every vehicle owned by him, file in the office of the secretary of state a statement of his name and address, with a brief description of the vehicle to be registered, including the name of the maker, factory number, style of vehicles and motor power on a blank to be prepared and furnished by such secretary of state for that purpose: the filing fee shall be two dollars.

Assignment of Numbers. Subdivision 2. The secretary of state shall thereupon file such statement in his office, register such motor vehicle in a book or index to be kept for that purpose, and assign it a distinctive number.

Numerical Seal. Subdivision 3. The secretary of state shall forthwith on such registration, and without other fee, issue and deliver to the owner of such motor vehicle a seal of aluminum or other suitable metal, which shall be circular in form approximately two inches in diameter, and have stamped thereon the words "Registered motor vehicle, No. _____, State of California," with the registration number inserted therein; which seal shall thereafter at all times be conspicuously displayed on the motor vehicle, to which such number has been assigned.

Re-registration of Vehicles. Subdivision 4. If the vehicle has been previously registered, the certificate issued thereon shall be returned to the secretary of state and in lieu thereof such secretary shall issue to said owner a registration seal containing the number of such previous registration upon payment of a fee of one dollar. Upon the sale of a motor vehicle, the vendor, except a manufacturer or dealer, shall within ten days, return to the secretary of state the registration seal affixed to such vehicle.

License Hanger.   Subdivision 5. Every motor vehicle shall also at all times have the number assigned to it displayed on the back of such vehicle in such a manner as to be plainly visible, the numbers to be in arabic numerals, black on white ground, each not less than three inches in height, and each stroke to be of a width not less than half an inch, and also as a part of such number the abbreviated name of the state in black on white ground, such letters to be not less than one inch in height.

Registration of Vehicles in Possession of Manufacturers and Dealers, Etc.   Subdivision 6. A manufacturer of or a dealer in motor vehicles shall register one vehicle of each style or type manufactured or dealt in by him and be entitled to as many duplicate registration seals for each type or style so manufactured or deal in as he may desire, on payment of an additional fee of fifty cents for each duplicate seal. If a registration seal and the corresponding number shall thereafter be affixed to and displayed on every vehicle of such type or style as in this section provided, while such vehicle is being operated on the public highways, it shall be deemed a sufficient compliance with subdivisions one, three, five and eight of this section, until such vehicle shall be sold or let for hire. Nothing in this subdivision shall be construed to apply to a motor vehicle employed by a manufacturer or dealer for private use or for hire.

Fictitious Registration Seals or Numbers.   Subdivision 7. No motor vehicle shall be used or operated upon the public highways after thirty days after this act takes effect which shall display thereon a registration seal or number belonging to any other vehicle, or a fictitious registration seal or number.

Motor Vehicles Not Complying With This Act.   Subdivision 8. No motor vehicle shall be used or operated on the public highways after thirty days after this act takes effect, unless the owner shall have complied in all respects with this section, except that any person purchasing a motor vehicle from a manufacturer, dealer or other person after this act goes into effect shall be allowed to operate such motor vehicle upon the public highways for a period of five days after the purchase and delivery thereof, provided that during such period such motor vehicle shall bear the registration

number and seal of the previous owner under which it was operated or might have been operated by him.

Motor Vehicles Owned by Non-Residents.   Subdivision 9. The provisions of this section shall not apply to motor vehicles owned by non-residents of this state and only temporarily within this state, provided the owners thereof have complied with any law requiring the registration of owners of motor vehicles in force in the state, territory or federal district of their residence, and the registration number showing the initial of such state, territory or federal district shall be displayed on such vehicle substantially as in this section provided.

Speed.   Sec. 3. Subdivision 1. No person shall operate a motor vehicle on a public highway at a rate of speed greater than is reasonable and proper, having regard to the traffic and use of the highway, or so as to endanger the life or limb of any person, or the safety of any property; or in any event on any public highway where the territory contiguous thereto is closely built up, at a greater rate than one mile in six minutes, or elsewhere in any incorporated city and county, city or town at a greater rate than one mile in four minutes, or elsewhere outside of any incorporated city and county, city or town, at a greater rate than one mile in three minutes; subject, however, to the other provisions of this act.

Speed When Approaching Bridge, Dam, Curve or Descent.   Subdivision 2. Upon approaching a bridge, dam, sharp curve, or steep descent, and also in traversing such bridge, dam, curve or descent, a person operating a motor vehicle shall have it under control and operate it at a speed not exceeding one mile in fifteen minutes, and upon approaching a crossing of intersecting highways at a speed not greater than is reasonable and proper, having regard to the traffic then on such highway and the safety of the public.

Speed When Approaching Pedestrians or Draft Animals.   Subdivision 3. Upon approaching a person walking in the roadway of a public highway, or a horse or horses, or other draft animals, being ridden, led or driven thereon, a person operating a motor vehicle shall give reasonable warning of its approach, and use every reasonable precaution to insure the

THE BRUSH RUNABOUT. Model D 28

IMPERIAL GARAGE

(INCORPORATED)

Agents in Alameda County for Brush Runabout
Company of Detroit

AUTO AND GENERAL MACHINE WORK

STORAGE, RENTING AND SUPPLIES

Everything for the Auto   Open Day and Night

PHONE OAKLAND 5420

1224-1226 Webster Street   OAKLAND, CALIFORNIA

safety of such person or animal, and, in the case of horses or other draft animals, to prevent frightening the same.

Speed When Passing Draft Animals. Subdivision 4. A person operating a motor vehicle shall, at the request or on signal by putting up the hand, from a person riding, leading or driving a restive horse or horses, or other draft animals, bring such motor vehicle immediately to a stop, and, if traveling in the opposite direction, remain stationary so long as may be reasonable to allow such horse or animal to pass, and, if traveling in the same direction, use reasonable caution in thereafter passing such horse or animal; provided that, in case such horse or animal appears badly frightened or the person operating such motor vehicle is requested to do so, such person shall cause the motor of such vehicle to cease running so long as shall be reasonably necessary to prevent accident and insure safety to others.

Stop in Case of Accident, Etc. Subdivision 5. In case of accident to a person or property on the public highways, due to the operation thereon of a motor vehicle, the person operating such vehicle shall stop and, upon request of a person injured, or any person present, give such person his name and address, and, if not the owner, the name and address of such owner.

Public Highways May Be Used for Speed Tests or Races. Subdivision 6. Local authorities may, notwithstanding the other provisions of this section, set aside for a given time a specified public highway for speed tests or races, to be conducted under proper restrictions for the safety of the public.

Meeting Other Vehicles or Draft Animals. Sec. 4. Subdivision 1. Whenever a person operating a motor vehicle shall meet on a public highway any other person riding or driving a horse or horses or other draft animals, or any other vehicles, the person so operating such motor vehicle shall reasonably turn the same to the right of the center of such highway so as to pass without interference. Any such person so operating a motor vehicle, shall, on overtaking any such horse, draft animal or other vehicle, pass on the left side thereof, and the rider or driver of such horse, draft animal or other vehicle shall, as soon as practicable, turn to the right so as to allow

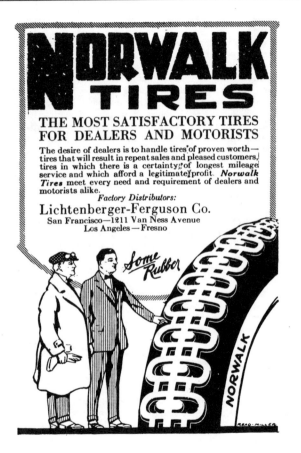

free passage on the left. Any such person so operating a motor vehicle shall at the intersection of public highways, keep to the right of the intersection of the centers of such highways when turning to the right and pass to the right of such intersection when turning to the left. Nothing in this subdivision shall, however, be construed as limiting the meaning or effect of the provisions of section three of this act.

Brakes, Bells, Horns or Other Signals. Subdivision 2. Every motor vehicle, while in use on a public highway, shall be provided with good and efficient brakes, and also with suitable bell, horn, or other signal, and be so constructed as to exhibit, during the period from one hour after sunset to one hour before sunrise, two lamps showing white lights visible within a reasonable distance in the direction toward which such vehicle is proceeding, showing the registered number of the vehicle in separate arabic numerals, not less than one inch in height, and each stroke to be not less than one-quarter of an inch in width, and also a red light visible in the reverse direction.

Speed Ordinances of the Local Authorities, Etc. Subdivision 3. Subject to the provisions of this act, local authorities shall have no power to pass, enforce or maintain any ordinance, rule or regulation requiring of any owner or operator of a motor vehicle any license or permit to use the public highways, or excluding or prohibiting any motor vehicle whose owner has complied with section two of this act from the free use of such highways, except such driveway, speedway or road as has been or may be expressly set apart by law for the exclusive use of horses and light carriages, or except as herein provided, in any way affecting the registration or numbering of motor vehicles or prescribing a slower rate of speed than herein specified at which such vehicles may be operated, or the use of the public highways, contrary to or inconsistent with the provisions of this act; and all such ordinances, rules or regulations now in force are hereby declared to be of no validity or effect; provided, however, that the local authorities of incorporated cities and counties, cities and towns may limit by ordinance, rule or regulation hereafter adopted the speed of motor vehicles on the public highways on condition that such ordinance, rule or regulation shall also fix the same speed limitation for all other vehicles, such speed limitation not to be in any case less than one mile in six minutes and on further condition that such incorporated city and county, city or town shall also have placed conspicuously on each main public highway where the boundary of such municipality crosses the same and on every main highway where the rate of speed changes, signs of sufficient size to be easily readable by a person using the highway, bearing the words "Slow down to _____ miles" (the rate being inserted) and also an arrow pointing in the direction where the speed is to be reduced or changed, and also on further condition that such ordinance, rule or regulation shall fix the penalties for violation thereof similar to and no greater than those fixed by such local authorities for violation of speed limitation by any other vehicles, which penalties shall, during the existence of the ordinance, rule or regulation, supersede those specified in section six of this act, and provided further that nothing in this act contained shall be construed as limiting the power of local authorities to make, enforce and maintain further ordinances, rules or regulations affecting motor vehicles which are offered to the public for hire.

Speed Regulations Governing Motor Vehicles in Public Parks or Parkways, Etc. Subdivision 4. Local authorities may, notwithstanding the provisions of this act, make, enforce and maintain such reasonable ordinances, rules or regulations concerning the speed at which motor vehicles may be operated in any public park or parkways, but in that event, must be signs at each entrance of such park and along such parkway, conspicuously indicating the rate of speed permitted or required, and may exclude motor vehicles from any cemetery or grounds used for burial of the dead.

Suits for Damages Account Injuries to Person or Property. Subdivision 5. Nothing in this act shall be construed to curtail or abridge the right of any person to prosecute a civil suit for damages by reason of injuries to a person or property resulting from the negligent use of the highways by a motor vehicle or its owner or his employe or agent.

Registration of Chauffeurs. Sec. 5. Subdivision 1. Every person hereafter desiring to operate a motor vehicle as a chauffeur shall file in the

office of the secretary of state, on a blank to be supplied by such secretary, a statement which shall include his name and address and the trade name and motive power of the motor vehicle or vehicles he is able to operate, and shall pay a registration fee of two dollars.

Assignment of Number.   Subdivision 2. The secretary of state shall thereupon file such statement in this office, register such chauffeur in a book or index to be kept for that purpose, and assign him a number.

Numerical Badge.   Subdivision 3. The secretary of state shall forthwith, upon such registration and without other fee, issue and deliver to such chauffeur a badge of aluminum or other suitable metal which shall be oval in form, and the greater diameter of which shall not be more than two inches, and such badge shall have stamped thereon the words: "Registered chauffeur No. _____, State of California," with the registration number inserted therein; which badge shall thereafter be worn by such chauffeur pinned upon his clothing in a conspicuous place at all times while he is operating a motor vehicle upon the public highways.

Badge Can Not Be Used by Other Persons.   Subdivision 4. No chauffeur, having registered as herein provided, shall voluntarily permit any other person to wear his badge, or shall any person while operating a motor vehicle wear any badge belonging to another person, or a fictitious badge.

Chauffeurs Must Comply With This Act.   Subdivision 5. No person shall operate a motor vehicle as a chauffeur upon the public highways after thirty days after this act takes effect, unless such person shall have complied in all respects with the requirements of this section.

Penalties for Violation of Provisions of this Act.   Sec. 6. Any person violating any of the provisions of this act shall be deemed guilty of a misdemeanor, and upon conviction thereof shall be punishable by a fine not exceeding one hundred dollars or by imprisonment not exceeding thirty days, or both, for the first offense; and punishable by a fine of not less than fifty dollars or more than one hundred dollars, or imprisionment not exceeding thirty days, or both, for a second offense; and punishable by a fine of not less than one hundred dollars or more than two hundred and fifty dollars or imprisionment not exceeding thirty days, or both, for a third or subsequent offense.

AN ACT

To add a new section to the Penal Code, to be numbered Section Four Hundred and Ninety-Nine B, relating to the unauthorized taking for temporary use or operation of automobiles, bicycles, motorcycles and other vehicles.

Approved by the Governor, March 18, 1905

The people of the State of California, represented in Senate and Assembly, do enact as follows:

Section 1. A new section is hereby added to the Penal Code, to be numbered four hundred and ninety-nine b, to read as follows:

499b. Any person who shall, without the permission of the owner thereof, take any automobile, bicycle, motorcycle, or other vehicle, for the purpose of temporarily using or operating the same, shall be deemed guilty of a misdemeanor, and upon conviction thereof, shall be punished by a fine not exceeding two hundred dollars, or by imprisonment not exceeding three months, or by both such fine and imprisonment.

COUNTY ORDINANCES REGULATING SPEED OF AUTOMOBILES.

In most of the counties, the state law regulating speed of automobiles prevails; there are a few, however, in which ordinances are in force modifying the speed laws as laid down by the state. Following are those in which such ordinances are in effect:

San Mateo County, 15 miles per hour.

Merced County, 15 miles per hour.

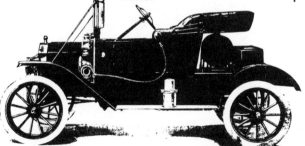

Monterey County, 15 miles per hour.

Stanislaus County, 15 miles per hour.

The above refers to all public highways without the limits of cities and towns.

These limitations would seem to be in conflict with Subdivision 1, Section 3, Chapter 612, of the Statutes of the State.

In Sonoma, as well as in some of the other mountainous counties, there exists an ordinance substantially as follows:

On all mountain roads, the driver of an automobile or motor vehicle, upon arriving within three hundred (300) feet of any vehicle propelled by animal power, and proceeding in opposite direction, shall immediately cause the automobile to take the outside of the grade and to immediately stop and remain stationary and noiseless so long as it may be necessary to allow said vehicle to pass or get out of the way.

The End